Up In the Sky

by Julie Larson

 NATIONAL GEOGRAPHIC  Hampton-Brown

National Geographic and the Yellow Border are registered trademarks of the National Geographic Society.

National Geographic School Publishing
Hampton-Brown
www.NGSP.com

Printed in the USA.
Quad Graphics, Leominster, MA

ISBN: 978-0-7362-7998-7

17 18 19   10 9 8

Acknowledgments and credits continue on the inside back cover.

See the clouds.

They are low.

See the stars.

They are bright.

See the planets.

They are high.

See Earth. It is home.